TWENTY WAYS TO FIND HOW TO FIND AND LAND
FREELANCE WRITING GIGS

Chapter 1

How do I make money writing? Are there other
ways to find and land freelance writing jobs?
I've asked these questions as a beginning
freelance writer and tried to find practical
ways to jumpstart my writing career. Needless
to say, some of those ways were more helpful
to me than others. For example, a few ways
were less time-consuming and more direct than
others. In upcoming chapters, I've discussed
just about all of these ways. You can pick

and choose a way or option that will work for you at any point and try it out. All of these ways take time to implement. But once you've found a way that works for you, feel free to implement it as many times as you like and make some money. Or combine two or more ways to implement. Whatever you choose, know that you will make some money at some point.

Ready? Set? Let's begin!

A SHORT INTRODUCTION

Welcome to the writing community! You
love to write and

A Short Introduction

Welcome to the writing profession! You love to write and want to find ways to break into the field. Let me be the first to let you know that you can and will make money writing at some point and only need ways to begin.

You will find twenty of those ways in the pages of this book. All you'll have to do is pick one or a combination of two or more ways and use them to customize your path to a profitable writing career.

Ready to take the plunge? Great!

Just dive right in!

, Check the IMP

The IMP is a reference that you may find in your library. It contains names and addresses

of publishers and editors. A few of those
publishers have new names as a result of their
becoming a part of a larger conglomerate. Look
through the pages and jot down names and
addresses of editors to contact with a brief
letter of inquiry. Remember that many of the
larger and well-known publishers require
agented submissions.

. Check the Writer's Market

The Writer's Market is another reference that
you may consult for free at your library or
purchase on your own for around twenty-five
dollars or so at bookstores. The Msrket is
published yearly and contains information on
book and magazine publishers who are
interested in receiving ideas and/or
manuscripts from writers. The Market also
features articles on getting your work out
there and earning money from your words.

Its entries include names of publishers and the type of work they wish to receive, the pay, and their response time. Also, the Market can save you a lot of wasted time and effort researching markets that are receptive to writers. You'll probably find a treasure trove of markets for your work.

. **Check reference books on writing**

Writing references are frequently overlooked sources of writing gigs and can be found in libraries or bookstores.

In addition to hints and suggestions for locating markets, these books frequently include names and locations of markets that you may contact and submit work to. In older references, this information will likely be outdated, but is handy for specific details. On the other hand, newer writing references are more likely to mention updated nemes and addresses of useful contacts.

. **Check your online phone directory for names and addresses of businesses that may be able to use your writing skills.**

Doing this helped me to land a gig that lasted two weeks and supplied me with a paycheck for each week. Best of all, landing this gig was relatively quick and easily done.

To land this gig, I made a list of ten local businesses, including print shops and local publishers that could probably use my skills. Then I called each business, briefly introduced myself and asked them if they could use help in proofreading or copyediting. Although nine businesses said "No thanks," one local pubisher said "yes" and invited me to take a short test onsite. The test was timed

Comment [DZ]:

and included about 15 items whose numbers and/or spelling matched or didn't match. I had to indicate matching items in that simpls test and passed it and got the job. This way, or option, is especially useful in locating a part-time temporary job in a hurry.

. Identify a common problem and write an article or book about it.

What emergency have you experienced lately and how did you deal with it? What solution worked for you and how? For example, how did you manage to find a good plumber in a short time who actually showed up and charged a reasonable fee for diagnosing and fixing a problem? And how did you prepare an excellent meal on short notice for unexpected company? What

Foods did you prepare and serve? What recipes did you use?

What would you remember to do or avoid doing in a future scenario and why? What foods do you tend to keep at home just in case? You can probably think of other good examples and describe how you dealt with each in an article or book. If you write a series of articles on that problem, you likely have enough work to fill a book! Check the Writer's Market and make a list of suitable magazines or book publishers to contact.

. Check ads in writer's magazines for jobs.

While there isn't usually a lot of job opportunities, it's still possible to find and respond to one. This is a numbers game, as a given ad has also attracted hundreds of applicants.

Responding to ads is like playing the lottery, and for that reason, you will want to avoid ads as much as possible. You may have better odds of landing something if you respond to ada in trade magazines, such as *Wtiter*.

. **Run your own ad**

Do you have related skills in indexing? Copyediting? Editing? What training do you have and where did you obtain it? How much are you charging and in how much time can you complete the job? Likely opportunities are available at publishers' offices, especially publishers that specialize in your field, such as accounting, nursing, etc.

. **Complain for dollars**

Have any of your complsint letters yielded desired results? Do you have a way with words and can help others get good results? In that case, you might consider running an ad that

Brings interested clients who need results with their complaints. You can offer to help them write letters that effectively state a given complaint that leads to a solution!

. Become a ghostwriter

A ghostwriter helps others to develop, write and complete a book project. You can write for individuals, professionals and companies. Before doing any work, discuss terms, deadlines, and pay and put them in writing, especially for individuals. On the other hand, companies tend to treat ghostwriters professionally and pay much better. These companies also have a variety of available projects, but rarely advertise their needs. Writers whose **expertise** in certain merchandise, electronics, professions in finance and education will likely qualify as ghostwriters.

. **Start a blog.**

As an expert in a given field, such as teaching or caring for pets, you may wish to try your hand writing a blog. Once your blog is several months old, or preferably a year old, you can submit it to sites as blogvertise, which can assign you to write a short post on a related product or service for a epecified sum of money, such as 20 dollars per post.

. Write letters for your favorite charity or charities

Chances are, you are familiar with one or more charities and share their passion of rescuing animals, helping veterans or victims of diseases as cancer, diabetes, Alzheimers, etc. Among these charities, common activities include fund raising

And raising awareness. Frequently, these charities need help in writing letters soliciting funds, articles and brochures and need good writers. In the beginning, you can offer your writing services for free, and with any luck, you'll land a writing gig that will pay off nicely. In any case, contact one or more charities and find out if they can use good writers such as yourself. You may be pleasantly surprised!

. Become a technical writer.

Do you have training and work experience in automotive issues, plumbing, electrical matters, teaching or in troubleshooting smartphone, computer and tablet problems? Can you write clearly? If so, you may be able to land a writing gig with a publisher who specializes in these fields and needs help in editing and writing instruction manuals and books. Of course, you should be familiar with a field's jargon or lingo and use it appropriately. In other words, you should ideally be an

Expert in that field and write about its aspects clearly and interestingly.

. Create and teach a course in your favorite subject or expertise.

Got a topic or subject that you just can't
stop discussing or helping others do? Why not
create a course on some aspect of that subject
or topic, sharing your knowledge of how to
break in, solve, implement, or fix? You can
offer it for free or pay online or at a
continuing education facility, such as a
college or community college.

. **Write articles for your local newspaper.**

True, most, if not all papers, rely on staff
writers in various areas such as travel,
health, finance and entertainment and
employment. At the same time, though, To find
a writing gig, create an article idea and
explain it to one of the paper's specialty
editors and why you're especially qualified
tor the gig.

Another idea is focusing on special pullout sections and checking for articles written by freelancers. If freelancers' articles are used, the paper uses freelancers and should be contacted for an article assignment. An important note/caveat is to write down your proposal before calling an editor, so you can present your proposal clearly and effectively. Try rhia and you may lend an article assignment. Pay for articles varies widely, ranging from a few dollars to a few hundred dollars. A lot depends on the paper and its geographical range.

. Contact an agency that specializes in placing freelancers like yourself.

Such agencies usually have close connections with publishers and companies that need and use freelance help. You'll need to visit that agency in person with a resume. You'll also need to demonstrate some proficiency in related skills in proofreading and copyediting and indexing. But once you're in, you're practically land a gig somewhere nearby whose pay is reasonable and dependable.

You may want to ask which agencies welcome or specialize in placing freelancers in your area on Google.

I also landed a gig that lasted nearly six months doing just that. And a fellow freelancer eventually landed a full-time copyediting position at that same company! She really needed that job, as she was down to her last seven dollars and couldn't afford to live without a job much longer.

. Join a writers' organization such as the National Writers Union

As a dues-paying member, you'll be able to expand your own network and become privy to job opportunities and have access to other writers and speakers who can help you find paying writing gigs. You may also gain access to health insurance and helpful written articles, pamphlets and white papers on various aspects of the writing profession.

. Start a newsletter on some aspect of your profession or expertise.

You choose your audience, such as laypersons or colleagues, issues of your newsletter's focus, practical solutions for saving time and money and ways to expand opportunities. You also get to decide how frequently your newsletter is published, its name and how much money it costs to subscribe to it.

. Let others know on social media that you are a writer and what your writing specialty is. Are you an experienced business writer, for example?

Consider broadcasting your talents on Facebook, Twitter and LinkedIn. You never know until you try. This is almost like playing the lottery, in that to win it, you've got to be in it. Spread the word to people you are familiar with, such as your doctor, dentist, stylist and alumni magazine.

. Find and contact new companies.

Go to your library's reference section and ask the librarian where you can find information on any companies who have arrived or started up in your area. Also consider contacting your local chamber of commerce or your town's municipal offices. Read reports and posters regarding that company or companies and figure out where and how they may be able to use your services before contacting them directly.

. **Offer to proofread, edit and create sales materials for local and nearby businesses.**

Doing this involves cold calling in person with writing samples or offers to do the first project for free or at a reduced fee. You'll probably get a number of "no thank you's" but at the same time, you'll become closer to contacting that one business that agrees to use your services. All you need at this point is one business! If you do a good job, word will soon apread about your writing talents and over time, businesses will be contacting *you*!

www.ingramcontent.com/pod-product-compliance
Lightning Source LLC
Chambersburg PA
CBHW081142280526
45787CB00007B/3189

9 781505 823134